Horseracing From the Inside Out

Horseracing From the Inside Out

❖ ❖ ❖

Owning, Training, and Betting Thoroughbreds

VIN ROGERS

ISBN: 1542673682
ISBN 13: 9781542673686
Library of Congress Control Number: 2017900977
CreateSpace Independent Publishing Platform
North Charleston, South Carolina

Table of Contents

Introduction

I 'VE ALWAYS BEEN fascinated by horses; so beautiful, graceful, yet powerful and dangerous too, as anyone who's been stepped on by an equine pet will sadly testify. This love affair may have begun with amusement park pony rides, but certainly escalated when my horse-playing dad took me to fabled Saratoga Race Course early one August morning when I was an impressionable five or six.

Saratoga at 7:00 a.m.; horses nervously prancing along the inside rail of the Oklahoma training track on their way to their workouts – almost close enough to touch. Exercise riders whispering, humming to their mounts. In the middle of the track runners galloping down the stretch, rhythmically snorting, riders clucking, trainers' eyes glued to stopwatches; heady stuff indeed for a six-year-old.

When workouts finished – about 10:00 a.m. – we walked the manicured backstretch barns and fed carrots to stabled horses. (Hold the carrots in the *palm* of your hand – or you may lose a finger!) And then, the ultimate treat, breakfast at the backstretch kitchen; juicy omelets, unlimited horse talk.

The years rushed by; high school, college, work, family; little time for horses except for occasional visits to whatever track was convenient when time permitted. But childhood memories of Saratoga mornings never quite disappeared; horses were in my head *and* in my blood.

I'd had an exciting and rewarding career in higher education, specializing in Education – i.e., *what* should children learn? *How* should they learn it? How do we *know* what they've learned? I had teaching-research gigs at universities on both coasts and many in between, as well as overseas assignments that included most of Europe, Africa, and the Middle East.

So – at 62 – I decided to turn the page - retire early and pursue passions that had been set aside for years; and *horses* were at the head of the list. I became a serious rider, beginning my riding career with lessons at the University of Connecticut's equine center and competed in local hunter-jumper events. Later I became an owner; first of saddle horses, but eventually and inevitably, of thoroughbred racehorses.

But long before my ownership experience, I dabbled in handicapping. My dad after all was a bettor; but he was a *connections* guy – a buddy of Hall of Famer trainer Sunny Jim Fitzsimmons. He had met Fitz at Belmont many years ago. A friendship blossomed and Dad was informed from time to time of ready FitzSimmons runners. I didn't have "connections"; but I *did* have an interest in the data, the analysis, the challenge of handicapping; so dabbling gradually grew to obsession; speed, pace, form, class – surely the handicapping puzzle could be solved if one worked long enough and hard enough on its solution.

I approached handicapping asking the same fundamental questions I'd asked about children's learning; how do *horses* learn? How do good trainers teach their charges? What is it they're teaching, and most importantly to the handicapper, how well were lessons learned?

These curiosities led to serious study of both the equine athlete and of the wisdom of competent trainers and handicappers. The years produced a body of writing about what I'd learned; and much of that work has appeared in *HorsePlayer magazine;* a journal committed to giving horseplayers everywhere a voice, to the well-being of grooms, hot walkers, track maintenance workers, and starting gate crew; most importantly, to the health and welfare of horses.

(My horse addiction also led to the publishing of two children's books *Sunshine Mary* – the story of a talented but reluctant runner, and *Midnight*, a racetrack mystery.)

This book is presented in six sections: Part I focuses on the horse itself; its nature, characteristics and idiosyncrasies. Part II describes my years as a thoroughbred *owner*; the highs and inevitable lows of horse ownership. Part III emphasizes my experience as handicapper; what I've learned after years of study and analysis. Part IV focuses on random events at the track that convey something of the flavor of racetrack culture. Part V is a tribute to the guy that got much of this story started; a 14-year-old chestnut quarter horse named Joey.

Part I: The Horse

❖ ❖ ❖

Handicapping: The Theory of Everything
-or-
(Why Our Meticulous Analyses Get Screwed Up So Often!)

Consider this common scenario: Joe Horseplayer is analyzing past performances for a claiming, dirt sprint at Aqueduct inner track. He knows his stuff: inner track favors speed – the horse he likes (let's call him "Mystery") has good early kick, wire-to-wire last – qualifies on class, connections, affinity for this track. Joe has viewed replays of Mystery's last two races and all the pieces fit. This guy should win.

But – Mystery does *not* win. He gets out of the gate okay; no trip issues – is on the lead briefly; then fades, finishes fourth in noticeably slower time than his most recent races.

Joe is understandably perplexed. He suspects drugs, larceny. He checks and rechecks his analysis; then berates himself for, perhaps, overemphasizing speed figures and track bias. *Next time,* he thinks, *pay more attention to class – or pedigree – or something else.*

But Joe's methodology was *sound*! The fault, dear Brutus, lay not in Joe's numbers but rather in the mind, the personality of this complex creature we call the HORSE.

Many years ago I wrote a children's book about a racehorse called *Sunshine Mary*. The inspiration for the book came from a piece I'd read in the *Daily Racing Form:* Sunshine Mary had raced 14 times and finished *last* in 11 of her races; and next to last in the other three. *But* – she continued to run eye-popping workouts on a daily basis!

How to explain this mystery? As a horse owner and rider, I knew a bit about equine behavior; thus this explanation for Sunshine Mary's performance appeared in the book: (remember, it's a *children's* book!)

"Suddenly she felt alone and a little frightened. She did not like running out there on the track by herself. It seemed like one of her lonely morning workouts. But then she heard the clippety-clopping of the horses behind her. She saw them running close together, and she could feel the thunder of their hooves on the track. Sunshine Mary slowed down. Soon one horse, then another, then another, and then another horse caught up with her. Then Sunshine Mary was surrounded by horses. She felt warm and safe as they gathered around her. She galloped easily and happily along until the race was over. This time Sunshine Mary didn't finish last – but, of course, she didn't finish first either." [1]

I think I was, quite innocently, *on to something!*

I've read most of the experts on thoroughbred horseracing analysis; Beyer, Free, Fotias, Scott, Crist, Davidowitz, Friedman, Meadow – and others. My 3x5 card notes, laid end to end, might stretch to Chicago.

These are smart guys; experienced guys – and I've learned an enormous amount from them. But – there is one *huge* gap in the handicapping literature I've read; insight into the *mind* of the thoroughbred racehorse

Horses have, of course, been ridden, trained, and observed for centuries; the Mongols on the Asian Steppes, the ancient Greeks and

---

1 Vin Rogers, *Sunshine Mary* (Middletown: Weekly Reader Books. 1983), 28.

Romans – and – in the 19th century, the father of modern horse breeding and understanding - perhaps the first "horse whisperer" – the legendary Federico Tesio.

Tesio and many others were interested in the horse's mind as well as its body. What goes on in a horse's mind – its personal, social, and emotional conformation can have an enormous effect on its physical performance.

I've spent the last two or three months delving into the fascinating field of horse psychology. I found a number of helpful references and finally settled on four recent sources: J. Warren Evans' *"Horses: A Guide to Selection, Care and Enjoyment"*; Robert Miller's *"Understanding Ancient Secrets of the Horse's Mind"*; Eunice Rush's *"Know You, Know Your Horse"*; and most importantly Kerry Thomas's *"Horse Profiling: The Secret to Motivating Equine Athletes."*

Rush and Morrow emphasized the similarities between human right brain-left brain social style traits, i.e., horses can be patient or impatient, subservient or dominant, compliant or assertive, confident or uncertain.

Evans divides horses into five major temperament types: quiet, interested, nervous, stubborn, and – sometimes – treacherous. Miller's *Ancient Secrets of the Horse's Mind* include the secrets of:

1. Flight, i.e. flight as a horse's primary survival behavior.
2. Perception; constantly on the lookout for danger.
3. Memory – infallible- forgets nothing!
4. Dominance hierarchy; e.g., some horses attempt to control the movement of their peers.

Kerry Thomas's work, however, is seminal to this discussion because he, far more than the others, relates his knowledge of and experience with equine athletes' psychology to the thoroughbred racehorse.

Thomas's focus is on the study of the emotional conformation of the individual and its relationship to the herd; i.e., "the everyday behavior and interaction that occurs within the intricate social order of the Equine circle (herd)."

I recently obtained a short, informal paper coauthored by Thomas and Peter Dent from Bloodstock Research Information Services in Lexington, Kentucky. They observe in their introductory paragraph "One of our long-term goals is to change the way people look at races...the study of equine communication, they write, "is like opening a window to the invisible."

Some on-track examples from the Thomas-Dent paper:

1. A horse whose vision is restricted by wearing blinkers for the first time overcompensates by turning its head to see the world around it (the other horses in the herd) disrupting the efficiency of its forward motion.

2. A horse seeks the comfort of movement with another horse. Buddy-up horses are dependent on another horse for safety, direction and rhythm of motion.

3. Some horses will prefer to be near the back of the field early in a race in order to read the other members of the group's intentions. They are, in fact, sizing up the field and determining where they want to go.

4. A horse engages in a pace duel with one other horse, not thinking about the rest of the field, the length of the race, or anything else but that one-on-one struggle.

5. One horse infringes upon another horse's comfort zone. Picture an invisible egg surrounding each horse. The size of that egg is dependent on the individual horse. Some horses shy from space infractions, some feed off of close contact.

These sorts of observations do not appear in the data provided by Brisnet, the *DRF*, Time Form, or any other data source commonly used by handicappers.

So – what to do? Most of us are not equipped for the sophisticated analyses of Thomas and Dent. Horses and their behavior are, after all, their life's work.

The famous (or infamous depending on your point of view) Secretary of Defense under President George W. Bush, Donald Rumsfeld, had it about right when, commenting on the complexities of international affairs, he explained there are:

1. Known knowns (things we know now)
2. Known unknowns (things we know we do not know)
3. Unknown unknowns (things we don't know we do not know)

For the handicapper, "known knowns" – things we know now – include a horse's average speed, its distance and surface preferences, the quality of its workouts, etc.

"Known unknowns" include the horse's potential trip, its physical health on given day, its ability (or lack of) to carry an added five pounds today, how it will react to starting from an inside (or outside) post for the first time, etc.

"Unknown unknowns" – for most of us – for the average horseplayer – include the sorts of interactions and behaviors described in Thomas and Dent's on-the-track examples. We are, essentially, helpless here.

Perhaps the best advice is to:

1. Recognize that nothing works *all* the time. Expect your most insightful analyses to be wrong from time to time.

2. *Do* check Trip's (charts and/or videos) when things *don't* work out, i.e., what happened during a given race? My analysis was sound – but did the trip make my numbers irrelevant?

3. Try to eliminate as many variables - "known unknowns" - as possible. For example, one might (as I do) limit one's play to non-maiden, six-furlong dirt sprints (Thomas believes that the shorter the race, the less opportunity for a group herd-based dynamic to develop) at Belmont, Aqueduct or Saratoga – tracks where I am familiar with surface idiosyncrasies, trainers, and jocks.

4. *Read* people like Thomas, Rush, and the others; can't hurt. You won't become an expert, but you will know more than you did before – and perhaps become most tolerant of your inevitable handicapping "errors."

Why We Lose

I WROTE A piece in a recent issue of *Horseplayer* ---title "Handicapping – The Theory of Everything." It focused on Kerry Thomas' research on handicapping problems caused by horses' *herding* instinct, i.e., "a horse seeks the comfort of movement with another horse; some horses prefer to 'buddy up'"; stay close to others – they feel safer this way. Clearly, this equine characteristic causes trouble for handicappers; no handicapping tool I know of factors this idiosyncrasy into its analysis.

I want now, however, to *expand* on that piece; to discuss a number of *other* equine characteristics that sometimes get in the way of our most thorough handicapping efforts.

Horesplayers have lengthy lists of explanations for losing wagers; lousy ride by jock, track playing too fast (or slow), pace too fast (or slow), Trainer X is a "lab trainer" – you've heard them all and more; and any or all may be valid explanations for our handicapping failures *some* of the time. But we've only touched the tip of the handicapping iceberg!

I've written (in *Horseplayer Magazine* "I'm About Even") of my experience as a thoroughbred *owner;* but I've never discussed my time as horseman, rider, and owner of four saddle horses (one, an off-the-track thoroughbred) during my two decades as a competitive hunter-jumper rider.

During those wonderful years, I learned of course to *ride* – but more importantly, I learned *horses*!

I did my share of stall mucking, feet picking, grooming, braiding manes and tails, and tidying up after a Niagara-like piss from Joey or Benny (barn names). I should add that there was a lot of hugging and petting going on, as well as mostly inane one-way conversations.

But graduation day came when my trainer told me it was time to learn to clean Joey's *sheath*.

Smegma – a collection of dirt and excretions – builds up inside a male horse's sheath. It must be removed periodically for the horse's health. This entails lubrication, then sliding your hand inside and up the sheath and carefully, gently removing the smegma.

It was tough – but I did it. Probably among the proudest moments of my life. I knew I had arrived; I could now call myself a *horseman*!

The horse is a complex, often bewildering, erratic, sensitive and wary creature. It sees both forward and backward; hears sounds a mile away, feels vibrations in the ground it stands on. It loves the familiar and dreads the unknown.

The next time you view a race – either on TV or at the track – watch carefully as the field – *any* field – experienced runners or maidens – approaches the starting gate. Remember; they've been there many times in both their schooling and/or racing experience. Yet one backs away; another plants its feet firmly in the ground and must be pushed and pulled into its stall by a locked-arms horse-savvy gate crew.

Once in the stall, some find reasons to object to their confinement; they wiggle and squirm enough to cause the jock to dismount. Again, they've been in the gate many times – it's *not* a new experience. Yet, from a given horse's point of view on a particular day, all may not be well.

So – *why* does this happen?

Perhaps on race day a new groom showed up at 5:00 a.m.; rare, but it happens. A strange face, an odd sound, a new smell – for some horses, a troubling experience; for others, all in a day's work.

Similarly the voices, smell, and especially the touch of a given gate crew member may be perceived as threatening by some horses; for others, a nearby spectator in a too-bright (for that horse) red sweater distracts, as may unexpected and unusual shadows gathering as the field loads for the afternoon's late races.

Once the race has begun, a dirt (or turf) track that looks like any other – indeed, a surface the horse has run on before – somehow feels different today. To a horse, all jocks are not equal and it may respond positively or negatively to each riders' idiosyncrasies.

(And – sometimes – *really* – on a given day and just like you – they simply wake up feeling crappy!)

These acute senses and sensitivities, of course, explain both their evolvement and survival during their centuries of existence on this planet.

A few weeks ago, I saw a horse unseat its rider early in a race at Belmont. His ears went up rather than down, and he quickly ran through the field, took the lead, and kept it to the finish.

Some horses *do* appear more ready to run on *any* given day than others. They are focused, less distracted, and appear to welcome the competitive experience; and they do so consistently. For me, that is the ultimate definition of that ephemeral term, "class." Some horses have it, many don't. Identifying those runners may be the key to success or failure at our game.

So – before a race is run, your analysis seems valid; all or most of the pieces fit – speed, class, pace, connections…but your horse finishes up the track! You berate yourself; what did I miss, where did I go wrong?

To paraphrase Cassius in *Julius Caesar*, "The fault, dear horseplayer, lies not in our stars, but in the horse's head…"

Losses are not always our analytical fault. What happens on a given day – from the time a horse awakens, feeds, is groomed, defecates, urinates, hears, smells, sees and feels – any or all may affect today's performance. *No* handicapping tool – not Brisnet, DRF, Thorograph, Predictaform, the Sheets – can factor the horse's nature into its predictions.

Having said all of this, it's amazing that we sometimes – perhaps enough of the time – get it <u>right</u>! Some days, all of the pieces <u>do</u> fit, and of course, that's what keeps us in the game.

In the Money

IT WAS AUGUST, 1978: temperature 92°, humidity 80%. Ed Smith (a fictitious name) and his wife Mindy were attending a yearling sale at Ocala; they wanted to buy a racehorse. Ed managed a small barn in Maryland; perhaps eight or ten horses; nothing like Pletcher, Baffert or Zito, but not the end of the line, either. His barn housed two or three steady allowance types, one minor stakes filly, four claimers, and a groom who had nowhere else to sleep.

Any horseman will tell you that you mustn't fall in love with the first horse you see if you're looking to buy. It's easy to do, happens often, and usually ends badly. But they *did* fall in love; and why not? Hip #155's breeding and confirmation were certainly acceptable though not exceptional, but he was a charmer; an athletic-looking, steely grey colt with bedroom eyes, perky ears and a nuzzler to boot. He was irresistible. He went at auction for a mere $1500. Since he had no name when purchased, we'll simply call him "Max."

I was deeply involved with horses as well at that time. I'd joined a syndicate of 45 dreamers, and our team purchased ten yearlings at an earlier auction in Lexington. All ten were vanned to Ocala where they would soon be enrolled in racehorse kindergarten. Ocala is, of course, horse country par excellence. It's home to some of the finest training facilities in thoroughbred racing, and an acknowledged Mecca for yearlings.

Ed, too, had made the decision to ship his new purchase to Ocala, and Max showed up one afternoon at the same facility our syndicate manager had chosen for our horses.

One morning, while I was watching a coal black filly being pampered by a groom old enough to have picked Seabiscuit's feet, a forty-ish, baseball-capped, binocular-laden guy stopped to admire the filly. We introduced ourselves, chatted, and he suggested coffee - I agreed.

Ed and I were together at Ocala for about a week. The babies were learning how to become racehorses and we were there every morning at trackside to monitor their progress. I was content to be an observer, but Ed, a trainer himself, took a proactive role in Max's education. Max was, in every way, a perfect gentleman; popular with exercise riders, grooms, vets and farrier. He wasn't a spectacular mover, but was focused and efficient; worked 3 furlongs in a comfortable :38, 4 in a leisurely :52.

A few weeks later, school was out; time for Ed to ship Max home, get him acclimated to a new barn, continue his training, and eventually, if all went well, look for a suitable spot for his racing debut. That opportunity came in mid-May; a five-furlong sprint, $12,000 Maiden special for state breds at a major Eastern track.

With steady if not spectacular works, Max was a respectable 12-1 at post time. He finished fourth; the chart read "Dwelt at gate." His second race resulted in a fifth place finish; chart read "Clipped heels at 1/4 pole." Third race: no "dwelt," no "clipped heels," good start. Max ran in mid-pack and closed for third.

Ed, Mindy, and their team of grooms, hot walkers, and exercise riders wanted a win. Ed tried a change in riders, a change in distance - he added and subtracted blinkers. Results? Three more starts, no wins - but in the money every time.

Advice came from many quarters; mostly "Why not drop him into a maiden claimer?" But this Ed could not do; Max had become a family pet - his kids adored him. He could not take the chance of losing him via the claiming box. The Ed barn brain trust met to discuss their horse's future. He'd had seven starts; in the money five of the seven. They concluded that Max, as lovable as he was, was at best an ordinary runner with an unfortunate tendency to prefer racing with and among horses rather than duking it out alone either in front or in the rear. Mindy handled the barn's books, and in a quick review of Max's monetary history, pointed out that he had earned $14,625 so far in his freshman year with his five in the money performances.

"And how much has he cost us so far?" asked Ed. "I mean *everything;* feed, vet, workouts - how much?" Mindy turned to her books and calculator, clicked away, and reported that Max's total expenses for the racing year were not quite $3,650.

"You sure?" asked Ed. "Check those numbers again."

She did - they were indeed correct. Two weeks later, Max was entered in another maiden special - this time for a $16,000 purse.

It's the day of the race, Max is brushed, combed, and polished for the occasion. The barn's blue and white silks almost glow in the afternoon sun. His rider - I'll call him Joe - arrives. Ed puts a fatherly arm around the diminutive jock and they confer for an animated five minutes or so. Ed gives Joe a leg up, and Max heads for the track. Max is 4-1 on the board (the public can't resist backing a horse that has finished in the money six times).

The race goes off, Joe positions Max fifth from the rail, comfortably surrounded by runners on either side. At the 8th pole, Joe clucks, Max surges forward, passes two horses, and finishes a respectable third, earning about $1000 for his connections.

Max raced til he was five (an injury kept him off the track during his four-year-old season). He *never* made it to the winner's circle. He was a perfect 0 for 32, but his lifetime earnings box showed $56,000. Indeed, the grey charmer had more than paid his way in each of his competitive seasons. But, perhaps wisely, was never asked to face winners.

Max's story reminds me a little of the infamous Zippy Chippy.

Zippy became a national phenomenon during his 14 years of racing. Despite royal lineage (parented by Compliance and Listen Lady and a blood relative to Northern Dancer) he had lost 99 consecutive races when he went to the post for the last time on Friday, September 10, 2004, at the Northampton, Massachusetts fair.

A huge crowd showed up; he was everyone's sentimental favorite and was bet down to 7-2. The Zip never made a move and finished last; now a perfect 0 for 100. But Zippy's dismal record had brought both notoriety and big bucks to his connections. Max was never in Zippy's class; hard to beat no wins in 100 tries. Yet, he had followed a similar path, proving that mediocrity could indeed be made to pay off.

The legendary Vince Lombardi famously taught that "Winning isn't everything - it's the *only* thing."

Not always.

Part II: Ownership

❖ ❖ ❖

Racing Partnerships: One Man's Experience

I'VE WRITTEN ELSEWHERE of an earthy trainer who, on a gloomy day, during Aqueduct's winter meeting, gleefully predicted that my horse would "piss all over that bunch." He was right; our four-year-old mare won by an expanding six lengths. He was, in fact, the trainer for one of my earliest ventures into racing syndication.

I hope he's still delighting owners with his sense of humor, racing acumen, and most importantly, *availability*. I was especially impressed because, after all, I only owned 3% of my horse – I was a *partnership* owner in a relatively minor league syndicate at that; some claimers, a few allowance horses, but nothing of stakes quality.

We had some winners, more losers – we didn't close the books with a profit – but Mr. X succeeded where some others failed, i.e., he made you feel like you had just given him a million dollar yearling to train – you were, in his barn, a *complete* owner, with all the rights and privileges that title suggests.

(Not so in some of my other partnership experiences; more of that later.)

I joined my *first* partnership twenty-five years ago. (I'm now 88 – still handicapping – far more fun than Lumosity.) We purchased ten classy yearlings, sent them to Ocala for training, and eventually, brought them (all but one) to the races. From start to finish, this was a *good* experience.

Owners were informed almost daily of our horses' progress. We were warmly welcomed by our training staff at Ocala, where we watched the youngsters learn to be racehorses. Questions were asked and answered, and – when our horses got to the track – we had box seats, paddock visits that included jockey and trainer chats, and most of all, a trainer who assumed we were serious about this game and intelligent enough to discuss our horses' successes *and* failures when we visited the barn or track; this was, indeed, the way it ought to be.

A few years later, I invested a sizeable chunk of money in a large claiming barn; very successful trainer (we'll call him Trainer Y) – well over fifty horses under his tutelage. We were to claim up to five horses during the fall at a major Eastern track.

Horses ran and claims were made; our stable was in business.

The negatives? We had little contact with the trainer himself. On the other hand, we had *daily* contact with his assistant-in-charge of clients. We were informed of works, injuries, jock selections, and most importantly (and rarely in my partnership experience) of a race's likely scenario in very specific terms, i.e., "There's not much speed in this field – our inside post should give us a decent break; we expect to go wire-to-wire today." Even better, we received almost daily emails about the *other* horses in Trainer Y's large barn; horses *not* included in our partnership; an unexpected extra!

On the negative side, I had the experience that all claiming barns fear; we put in a claim for a horse that broke down at the head of the stretch; had to be put down. Hard to describe the depth of despair and sheer sadness I felt – but I guess that it's all part of our game. (At this writing, the rules have changed in some venues, i.e., the claimant is not responsible if their horse breaks down during the race in which he or she has put in a claim.)

Another positive experience involved my 5% investment in a two-year-old colt that seemed to have unlimited potential. This barn dealt *only* with well-bred and, therefore, expensive prospects; no claimers – *big* investment for me! Unfortunately, the colt never quite lived up to expectations, and we finally lost him in a low-level optional claimer.

The barn, however, won big!

Why?

Again, superb communications from barn to owner, royal treatment at the track when our horses raced, and most importantly, a trainer who – whether you were a 5% or 90% owner – welcomed you during barn visits and took the time to discuss our horses' progress and/or problems.

Partnership #5, however, can only be described as weirdly negative.

I had read a good deal about Trainer Z – another successful East coast claiming trainer. He was by reputation smart, articulate, and blessed with an infectious sense of humor. I'd been out of the game for a few years at that time and decided, on a whim, to give the barn a call. Much to my surprise, Trainer Z answered – in person! I was delighted; wonderful positive omen.

He said he'd be putting in a claim for a filly he'd had his eye on for a while – entered in a race to be run in two or three days. Would I be interested? "Think about it," he said - and "call me back if you're in – and if not, there'll be plenty of other opportunities down the road."

Man, I'd been chatting for twenty minutes with Trainer Z! If he's that accessible, a small investment might yield much more than mere $$$

I called back; said "Okay – count me in – I'll take 5% of the filly."

That was the *last* time I spoke to this guy; at the track, barn, or on the phone. Communicating duties were quickly passed on to a "stable manager"; *his* phone was perpetually busy! My horse might be running on Wednesday – but Monday and Tuesday would be spent collecting "not available at this time – will get back to you a.s.a.p." phone messages.

I know this doesn't seem possible, but by golly, it happened!

Partnership #6 – another negative – involved a trainer who fawned on his *individual* owners – while largely ignoring we partnership guys. We were second-class citizens; tolerated only because the barn needed our bucks to stay in business. No pre-race or post-race conversation, no time for talk about the barn or at workouts; he succeeded in making us feel like outcasts.

Partnership #7 was also, regrettably, negative. (This was largely my fault; no place for innocents in this game!) I had a small percentage of two horses in barn #7. The groups' manager called one spring morning and told a heartbreaking story about a partner with terminal cancer; simply had to unload his 10% ownership in one of the barn's runners – a productive, minor stakes horse – and "a great opportunity" for me. I could own 10% of the horse at a considerable discount.

You can guess the rest of this story; the horse had a strained ligament in its left front that would only get worse. He raced a few times, finished up the track, and was soon retired.

Yeah, there *are* people like that in our sport – I was naïve – beware!

A few years later, another experience, partnership #8. I was contacted by a barn whose trainer *Horseplayer* readers would quickly recognize; we'll call him Trainer W. Our phone conversation went something like this: "We have a four-year-old colt just flown to the States from Ireland - stakes quality – sky's the limit with this one. Are you interested? If so, let's arrange a meeting at the paddock entrance tomorrow – I'll fill you in on details."

It was August – Saratoga time. I've always been in love with Saratoga's paddock (who isn't?). I didn't have owner's credentials at the time and was denied admittance to horseracing Mecca, thus the invitation was especially appealing. I agreed. We met and entered the inner sanctum. Trainer W had a horse going in the upcoming race, so we admired the chestnut filly together, and chatted briefly with the jock.

Now, back to the Irish colt; if I wanted in, I must commit *today* – for reasons I've since forgotten.

I said I'd let him know that evening – but – fortunately – my subconscious mind kept repeating the mantra *"Don't* invest in *anything* the *must* be done *today."* I declined this "once-in-a-lifetime" opportunity. The Irish colt *never* got to the races.

There was *almost* a partnership #9, but not quite. I was contacted by a prestigious stakes-class barn - a new crop of two-year-olds had been purchased at the Keenland sales – would I be interested?

Turns out I *was.*

This barn was rapidly moving up, making its mark. A meeting was arranged: breakfast with Mr. A, the stable's founder and bossman, at Saratoga's delightfully Victorian "Reading Room" – just across from the track. I was dined (not wined - it was, after all, breakfast) given the stables' pitch – and was sorely tempted.

But – had to say "No"; just couldn't afford the pricetag – out of my league.

I still feel guilty about the breakfast.

So – nine partnerships; that's a *lot* of experience. Let me finish, then, with some advice to prospective partners:

1. Have realistic expectations. This is a tough game! Odds are that you're going to lose money – but – if you choose wisely – your on-track experiences will be well worth the price.
2. *Do* take the time to talk to current syndicate partners. (Ask the barn for names of four or five). Obviously, if a barn is reluctant to share partner names, steer clear of that outfit.
3. Check the barn's "past performances" – easily available on the internet. Where have they been racing? Types of races? Trainers?

What's the barn's win percentage? (Personally, I'd like something close to 20%).

4. Probably best to spread the risk, i.e., invest in a *cluster* of horses rather than staking everything on one horse's performance. It's often tempting to do so – but for the investor with limited resources, usually not a good idea.

5. *Don't* expect "sure things," "hot tips." My two examples, - the "piss all over this bunch" barn and the "early speed" outfit – were more exceptions than rule. Most of the stables I've been associated with are (with good reason) cautious about hyping their runners.

6. Where do you want your horses to race? Some partnerships race on the East coast, West coast, and in between. If you want to be at the track for your horse's races, visit the barn and watch the workouts, consider an outfit that concentrates on the tracks nearest you.

7. Are you looking for a Derby horse? Or do you simply want to be part of the action, i.e., get *inside* this exciting game, learn more about the breeding and training of race horses? Where you come down on this question should have a lot to do with your partnership choice.

8. Be wary of any barn that offers "All the excitement and privileges that go with owning your own racehorse...$500 will get you in the game...call...operators are standing by..." (I've *had* that phone call!) Common sense tells you that it just ain't so!

So – to partner or not? Up to you.

My feelings were made clear in the concluding paragraph of a recent piece I wrote for this magazine:

"...I was at last an *owner* – a genuine, horseshit-on-my-shoes, stepped-on-and-bruised, Owner! I watched my horses work on glorious August mornings at Saratoga, then fed them carrots in the barn; I visited the winner's circle at Monmouth, Aqueduct, Belmont, and Saratoga and hung out with the swells in the Saratoga paddock – yelled til I was hoarse when one of *my* runners hit the finish line first."

It's up to you.

I'm About Even...

I'M WALKING DOWN main Street one late September day and I spot Charlie W., an old horserace buddy of mine – hadn't seen him for two or three years. As he comes closer, I see that he looks a mess; hasn't had a shave or haircut for a while – jeans and sweatshirt stained, torn; the epitome of a guy down, down, down on his luck.

Charlie – where've you been? What's happening, man?

Hey, how YOU doin'? Last time I saw you we were trying to hit the pick six at Aquaduct.

Yeah – with the usual results. You still playin'?

Oh sure, sure.

How you doin'?

I'm about even.

Old story, but I think, an accurate description of an inveterate horse-player, i.e., most of us are a long, long way from being "about even."

My dad introduced me to the sport when I was five. A few visits to Belmont and Saratoga and I was hooked – the seed was planted. No carousel could compete with the sights, sounds, and even smells of the racetrack.

I can't remember much horseplaying activity in high school; more concerned then with jazz and girls. But the seed my dad planted grew some when I arrived "Far Above Cayuga's Waters," in Ithaca, New York for my freshman year at Cornell. Remember the faux off-track betting parlor in Redford and Newman's gambling masterpiece, *The Sting*? The director could have used the establishment in downtown Ithaca as a model. (This was fifty years ago; betting was illegal *anywhere* except at the track.) Whenever I had time (which wasn't often – classes were tough, profs demanding, studying 3-5 hours per day essential) I'd head downtown for some horseplaying action that included a hint of old-fashioned mafia-like mystery.

The formidable red oak door which led to the place had a fully-functioning peephole. Inside – scattered folding chairs, poster-patched walls, two betting windows manned by eye-shaded cigar-puffing ca-shiers and the steady drone of racing information… "Scratch #2, Here's Sandy from the 8th at Belmont…" heard over the joint's speaker. I'd usually end up putting five bucks on some favorite (hadn't become a handicapper yet) maybe double my money; but I think I went mostly for the illicit thrill that came with simply being there.

In any case, my college betting left me considerably far from "about even."

Racing took a back seat for the next twenty years or so. Graduate school, marriage, children, career – no time and often no place for racing action. But – after a series of teaching gigs at Syracuse and the Universities of Massachusetts and Minnesota, we finally settled at the University of Connecticut in bucolic Storrs. The kids were grown and gone; Aquaduct, Belmont, and best of all Saratoga were all in reach,

I'd occasionally motor down the Merritt Parkway for a day at one of the New York tracks – usually Belmont – but an August visit to Saratoga became a ritual. No need to dwell on the magic of the Spa in August – that's become a cliché. However, I'm certain that the owner-ship bug took a bite some August afternoon as I gazed at the gated, guarded, sanctuary that was the Saratoga paddock.

A year or so later, a piece in the *DRF* caught my eye. A Saratoga-based vet who treated the horses of a dozen or so of racing's top barns, was forming a racing partnership. The goal was to raise enough money to purchase eight or ten yearlings and, under his guidance (and with luck!) eventually get them to the races. I liked what I'd read – investigated further and decided that a $10,000 share was a reasonable way to begin an ownership career.

All went according to plan; the horses were purchased, trained at our base in Ocala, and eventually, all but one made it to the track. Even more impressively, eight of the ten <u>won</u> their maiden races – two on the same magical day at Monmouth!

So – I was now an *owner* – the paddock was no longer forbidden territory; box seats for our races – and a promising youngster named "Fighting Affair" entered in the Saratoga Special. We were on our way!

Fighting Affair finished second in the Special but suffered what was described as a minor bruise on his left front hoof. In time, the minor bruise became major. Six races later, he began an involuntary retirement. The other seven runners never got beyond allowance races. They were dropped into claimers, and eventually, all were gone – as was my $10,000.

Nothing "even" about that transaction.

A few years later I hooked up with another barn that featured a Hall of Fame trainer, P.G. Johnson; great guy, articulate, charming, really impressive. I signed up for another $10,000 which bought me a 10% share of a promising colt named "Call Me Anytime." We got a <u>big</u> win out of him at Saratoga, and I was walking on air for a while; but the euphoria faded along with "Call Me's" fractions. Within six months, he too was gone – as was my $10,000.

I cooled it for a few years. Ownership had not been kind to me and I was anything but "even."

Finally, now retired and looking for some wholesome retirement activity that would keep me interested, involved, and active, I turned again to horse ownership. This time I decided to go for broke – took 3% of a $200,000 colt by Empire Maker that might have Derby possibilities – name, Make History. The colt lived up to his pedigree's promise – trained well, super-quick works; then ran a <u>powerful</u> second at Belmont against a classy group of Maiden Specials. This performance caught the eye of a number of trainers and owners and one day the barn gets a call with an offer of $750,000 for our colt!

Hey, this is it – finally hit the jackpot – gonna get a hell of a lot more than "even" this time!

Not so fast, Vincent. The barn announced a conference call for Make History's owners – the proposed deal needed to be discussed and presumably approved by a majority of his owners. Turns out that History has a bad knee; the buyers would of course be entitled to a thorough vetting before the sale could be consummated – and the possibility of the sale going through was now nil.

"History" worked a few times, but it became clear that his racing days were over. He was retired to a partner's farm, and my six grand was retired as well.

Am I "about even"?

Not if you add up the bucks I've lost in these ill-fated ownership adventures.

But – but – man, I was an *owner* – a genuine, horseshit-on-my-shoes, stepped-on-and-bruised, Owner! I watched yearlings train at Ocala; I watched *my* horses work on glorious August mornings at Saratoga, then fed them carrots in the barn; I visited the winner's circle at Monmouth, Aqueduct, Belmont, and Saratoga, and hung out with the swells in the Saratoga paddock; had a pre-race chat with Jorge Chavez, and post-race analysis with P.G., met some wonderful folks along the way, yelled til I was hoarse when one of *my* runners hit the finish line first.

So – am I "about even"?

I think so.

Part III: Handicapping

❖ ❖ ❖

A Conservative's Approach
to Handicapping

THIS IS, AFTER all, the political season; debates, speeches, polls, accusations, denials, robocalls. This piece, however, has *nothing* to do with politics – and everything to do with the human personality; both genetically and as formed by the cumulative effects of one's life experience.

I wrote, in a previous HANA article ("The Theory of Everything") that I was "far more handicapper than gambler."

Let me explain: I am by nature and experience a fiscally conservative guy; child of the Great Depression.

Consider: I was the leader of my high school jazz band and a good enough trumpeter to be offered an on-the-road gig with the (then) famous Louis Prima band – man, that was tempting! But – ultimately – I decided that college was a safer bet. College career choice? Teaching. Can't get more conservative than that! I saved, invested prudently, and can honestly say (in my "golden years") I'm comfortable.

My interest in *horses* began early – but not at the racetrack. I'm talking amusement park ponies at age five or six, later, county fair horse shows, and later still (oddly) as a Cornell undergraduate, admiring both the horses and the horsemanship of the Big Red national championship polo team.

For me, at that time, horseracing was essentially the Kentucky Derby, Preakness, and Belmont – and occasionally – for some illicit fun – a visit to an illegal betting joint in downtown Ithaca during my undergraduate years.

Fast forward 15 or 20 years; I'm now a professor of Education at the University of Massachusetts in Amherst. Every summer in nearby Northampton, the county fair comes to town – and so does horseracing. Turns out that a guy who lives next door on pretty Pomeroy Lane knows a guy who trains horses – and he shares a "sure thing" entered in Saturday's feature race at the fair. The "sure thing" wins – and I begin to see horses in a different light, i.e., serious **money** was changing hands at the racetrack!

Next step - a visit to Saratoga – and I was hooked forever.

I evolved from horse "lover" to horse "player." I discovered the *daily racing Form*, Rogazin's "sheets", Andy Beyer on speed, Cary Fotias on pace, Bill Scott on form – and much, much more.

As an academic – serous scholar and researcher – I found this data compelling. I was, indeed, hooked; but not so much at the prospect of wining big bucks but rather on the challenge of making sense of the data itself. I believed that, if one tried hard enough – gathered the best data and put in the necessary hours, one *could* solve the equine puzzle. Making a "life-changing score" was never my goal. Hooray for the Rainbow Pick Six winners; I wish them well – but I'm playing a different game.

Most of us have seen the ubiquitous ads for brain games designed to sharpen and hone memory, focus, and attention; "Lumosity" comes quickly to mind. "One must exercise one's mind", the ads say, or risk inevitable mental deterioration.

My mind game focuses on the analysis of the wealth of data available to today's handicappers.

I use Brisnet's Ultimate past performances exclusively; they include both speed and hard to find pace figures, class and race ratings, trainer-jock stats, pedigree data, and more.

In addition – and at the click of a mouse – Twin Spires' "professional" site allows me to access a horse's *lifetime* record - *every* workout, *every* surface, *every* distance, *every* race. Charts and video replays? Available with another click. Similarly, career trainer and jockey stats appear; *fifty* trainer categories, e.g., turf routes, dirt sprints, first time Lasix, etc. Similar data is available for jockeys as well as comprehensive pedigree stats.

That's a *lot* of information – for many, data overload.

But I'm not analyzing *every* race.

I've learned, over time, where my strengths and weaknesses lie. Examples? I will *not* play turf races – I simply can't cope with the inevitable last minute cavalry charge – ten or more horses fighting for position around the far turn, bumping, forced wide, pinned on the rail, blocked – just doesn't work for me. Of course these conditions (large fields, crowded late runs) often produce monster pay-offs – but as I've said before, that's simply not my game.

Neither will I play maiden specials or claimers, races at distances longer than a 1 1/8, and for obvious reasons, races over fences.

So what's left?

Plenty!

I can almost always find two or three playable races each day at the tracks I frequent, i.e., Belmost, Aqueduct, and Saratoga. (Obviously, concentrating on the idiosyncrasies of two or three tracks should sharpen one's analyses.)

And – two or three races are really all I can handle! Watching replays, checking jock-trainer data, career works and races, etc. takes *time*! But that's okay with me - I need time to solve the puzzle- and it's the process of analysis itself that drew me into handicapping in the first place – it's what (at age 88) keeps me in the game.

Consider this scenario; I'm at the track – the horses are rounding the far turn, entering the stretch. The guy next to me is shouting "Come on with that 7!" Another guy is begging "the 3" to accelerate; still another tears his ticket, throws it on the ground, and mutters "The 8 didn't run a step."

By the time one of *my* horses hits the stretch, I know his name, his mom's and dad's names, maybe his grandma's and grandpa's names!

Win or lose, this old brain has been stimulated – and the old heart is thumping; it's the way I play the game.

The Amorphous "Class"

ANYONE REMEMBER THE now-defunct TV show, *"Horseplayers"*? Contest winning handicapping pros discussed winning and losing – and hinted – only *hinted* - at their favorite methods or angles – e.g.; a winning handicapper is asked *how* he picked a 15-1 shot in a key contest race. We eagerly await his wisdom, pen in hand.

"Class on the grass" he replies.

But what does he mean by "class"?

He *doesn't* elaborate; *no one* did on that show, as I remember it. (Perhaps that's why the network cancelled it only after five or six airings.)

What *did* he mean – what do we mean when we refer to a horse's "class"?

A BBC soccer announcer during a championship tournament, commented that "Form is fickle; class is permanent." Simply stated, some horses are born with the physical ability to compete at a higher level than others.

Fair enough – but as we shall see, not the whole story.

Readers of this magazine will be of course familiar with thoroughbred racing's four basic classifications, i.e. Maiden, Claiming, Allowance, and Stakes. But it is often the differences *within* those basic classifications that matter when analyzing class.

Those who watch the races on TVG are probably familiar with handicapper–announcer Rich Perloff. Rich usually handles Monday and Tuesdays' sparse racing fare, filling the time responding to fans' often insightful emails, and – more importantly – dissecting the *conditions* for a given race. For example: a one-mile, $5,000 claimer run this February at Laurel is "restricted to four-year-olds and up which have not won a race since August 8th, or which have never won four races." Rich would start his analysis by reminding his viewers that all $5,000 claimers are not the same. In this case, which horses *have* won a race before August 8th? And which horses *have* won three races? What was the quality of the three wins?

For many handicappers, this race is simply a $5,000 claimer. Perloff specializes in *condition analysis* which is, of course, a form of *class* analysis.

Brisnet's Ultimate Past Performances include numerical race and class ratings. Thus the handicapper may ignore the "conditions" so dear to Perloff's heart. These computer-based ratings compare the quality of horses competing in a given race – which horses they have beaten, which horses have beaten them.

Bris's Race Ratings quantify the *quality* of a given field, e.g., a race with a "race rating" of 115 is a tougher bunch than a field rated 112 – regardless of stated conditions. Thus, two $25,000 claiming races with similar internal conditions might differ significantly in terms of the ability of the horses competing in those races.

Similarly, Brisnet's *class* rating identifies the *quality* of a given horse's actual *performance.* Thus Horse X's last race might have a race rating of 112, while its performance in that race might be 115. Another horse in the same field might also have a 112 race rating, while its *class* or performance rating was a dismal 110. (Brisnet race and class ratings are calculated daily for every race run in North America. However, unlike Brisnet's powerful Prime Power ratings, there is, at this writing, no objective data to support the accuracy of these ratings.)

As far as I know, Brisnet is the only handicapping source that has attempted to *quantify* class; indeed, the first to suggest a radically different definition of class.

Let me suggest an alternate view of the concept that neither negates nor supports the views previously expressed – but was hinted at in my recent piece, "The Theory of Everything" (*Horseplayer*, October 2015).

I'm enjoying a lovely August afternoon at Saratoga. A race is in progress. The horses round the clubhouse turn and head for the back stretch. Suddenly, a rider is unseated. His horse (let's call him Mike) was racing two or three wide, within three lengths of the leader – clearly in contention – but, once the rider is thrown, Mike leisurely drifts toward the outside rail, and essentially, packs it in.

But occasionally – admittedly rarely – I've seen a remarkably different scenario. Another horse – we'll call him Jim – has the same experience, but Jim continues on, passes one, two, three horses, gets the lead and stays there. I have no idea what race or class rating, speed figure, etc., that Jim might have earned for that race, but it really doesn't matter – that was a *classy* performance.

Think of Zenyatta sizing up the field some twenty lengths behind as the other horses approach the stretch. Field size, pace, running position, (usually dead last) none matter. She'd start that incredible stretch run until she poked her head in front, race after race after race; *class* to burn!

Some horses will stumble or be bumped at the break and quit; others pull themselves together, ignore the trouble and run their race. A classless horse on the lead – often with superior speed figures – quits when challenged while a classy animal perseveres. Horses rounding the far turn in a race on grass are often involved in a rugby-like scrum with a half-dozen others; the classy ones ignore the rough stuff and carry on; others pack it in. (This may also apply to some jockeys!)

So - for me – a significant dimension of any notion of class must include the qualities of versatility, competitiveness, courage, stamina, and spirit; the will to win – qualities that separate the champion from the also-rans, both equine and human.

Handicapper's dilemma?

There ain't no way to quantify *this* notion of class.

But astute handicappers are doing what researchers would call "qualitative analysis" on a daily basis. I'm referring of course to *trip* handicappers; those who diligently study live races or replays to see *how* a race is run.

If one is focusing on New York racing i.e., Belmont, Aqueduct, and Saratoga – the readily available *charts* for those races are thorough, detailed, descriptions of *how* a race is run, written by experts who make their livings watching and describing races. I read them regularly and bow to their observational expertise; I cannot see what their experienced eyes see when they chart a race; the charts are my alternative to actually watching and analyzing races, either live or readily available replays.

(My experience with charts from other tracks, however, has been largely negative – minimal information – like comparing Tolstoy to Dan Brown.)

If trips and charts are too much for you, try paying close attention to the cleverly abbreviated, space-saving "comments" that appear at the end of a horse's running line in virtually all past performances.

Consider these examples:

6-7 w. upper; willingly
fell to face st. game
stk. btwn; resilient
bulled way out 4 w. upper
4 wide 3/8: never gave up
bid between: determinedly

Willingly, game, resilient – are synonyms for "class"!

Conversely, "empty" and "no match" suggest either serious form defects or a horse which badly needs class relief.

I should add that significant trip or chart observations quickly find their way into my efficient Brisnet "Stable Alert" site. So easy – no excuse not to use!

One last and very important source of qualitative data is available in the *DRF*'s "Closer Look" commentary, e.g. –

"Sweet Laurel had a start since some of the others last raced and in that one this gal was stuck on the fence and then battled hard…"

These observations by experienced, perceptive pros are welcome additions to the handicapper's arsenal.

One more suggestion: the astute "horse whisperers" who make paddock observations at some tracks – I think immediately of Caton Breder at Gulfstream and Maggie Wolfendale at Saratoga – might consider adding some degree of personality or temperament commentary to their helpful but mostly *physical* analyses.

In the meanwhile, digest those conditions, experiment with Brisnet's race and class ratings, and, if you're really stuck, resort to the completely undocumented, unscientific and incredibly simplistic Vin Rogers alternate method of class analysis, PURSE SIZE: the larger the purse, the tougher the field – Money Talks!

Good luck!

Accentuating the Negative: Ten Past Performance Red Flags

ANYTHING CAN HAPPEN in a horse race; remember the immortal Man O' War's monumentally unpredicted loss to the aptly named "Upset"? Horses who should win often lose; and horses that should lose sometimes win. Why? It's the nature (and charm!) of our game.

Nevertheless, most handicappers continue to search for clues – evidence – in a horse's past performance that will minimize the margin for error and thus produce a reasonable number of winners. It turns out, however, that the identification of potential winners is inextricably linked to the elimination of the most likely **LOSERS**.

So – who are the most likely losers? That depends on each handicapper's experience; but for me, the following are bright red flags:

Throw out:

1. Any horse wearing a bar shoe or aluminum pad. The equipment board is telling us that this guy's hurting.
2. Horses with three or more double-digit losses in a row in their most recent races; no excuses for three such dismal performances; current form is simply unacceptable.

3. Runners with odds of 20 to 1 or higher in their last three races. The public doesn't know everything, but it does know *something.*

4. Any horse with 15 or more starts with a record of only one win, but many seconds and thirds *and* (usually) a hefty and misleading earnings box. Don't be misled by ITM performances and earnings. These guys will very likely lose again.

5. Favorites which had double-digit losses in their last race. Jocks are aware they're riding well-bet horses; they know the public has included them in win, place, and show bets as well as supers and tris, etc. They will always do their best to get a win or ITM finish. When that *doesn't* happen, something's wrong.

6. Perennial losing closers (they always seem to need another 50 yards or so) and their counterparts, perennial faders. Even though their earnings and speed figures look good and they show many ITM finishes, they're money burners.

7. Older horses (five and up) coming off a one-year (or more) lay-off. Despite good works, connections, trainer stats, etc., they will almost always need more time.

8. An experienced horse which does not show *one* speed figure equaling todays' par in its past performances has little or no chance of winning, and clearly needs a class drop.

9. Experienced, capable dirt winners which have *never* raced on grass, returning after a lay-off *on grass.* The race is almost certainly a prep for a race down the road; a conditioner.

10. Finally, for those who use Brisnet past performances – throw out any horse that ranks 8 points or more below the *top* horse in Brisnet's Prime Power ratings. (Prime Power is a comprehensive

rating that combines speed, class, form, weight, and more into one powerful numerical rating.)

To repeat, rules are made to be broken and there will, of course, be exceptions. And throw-outs *can* and *do* finish ITM. Nevertheless, your ROI should increase if you incorporate all or some of these cautions into your daily handicapping routine.

Accentuating the Positive

WROTE A piece in a recent issue of Horseplayer called "Accentuating the Negative – Ten Past performance red Flags."

This piece deals with its opposite, *positive* angles.

I've found through the years that the most consistently successful positive angle is to bring a novice race-goer with you when you go the track. You will, of course, use your experience and expertise to analyze each race, while your friend will choose horses with cute names, long tails, (or maybe short) jazzy barn silks and, if she's a woman, good-looking jocks (ever seen a close-up Edgar Prado?)

This is a hopeless scenario for you, Joe Horseplayer. Your horse finishes up the track while the grey with the handsome rider wins handily at 10-1.

Barring regular assistance from novices, what *are* some positive counterparts to my negatives list that have, over time, proven helpful to me and to other veteran players? (I should add that I have no science, no data, to support these angles; they are culled from *my* experience at the track and from the collective experience of veteran horseplayers I've known or read.)

I react quickly – almost automatically – to my handicapping *negatives*. If a horse is listed as wearing an aluminum pad or bar shoe he is *out* – eliminated – no further analysis needed. Three or four double-digit losses in a row, no excuses, increasingly long odds – eliminate!

Not so with positives; they're far more complicated and certainly *not* automatic selections; positive angles must be considered holistically - e.g., if sudden improvement is a significant positive – and it is – what are the attributes of the *other* runners in the field?

I use my positives to call my attention to horses I might otherwise have overlooked; I examine *their* past performances more closely, perhaps reconsider a horse I might have ignored. I don't (and you probably don't either) follow them slavishly - e.g., a horse might have shown dramatic improvement in its last race; but if that improvement is followed by a six month lay-off, that angle really doesn't mean much!

Let's begin:

1. The obvious – and the cardinal sin of horseplayers who ignore it – the most dependable angle out there though it occurs rarely – *ONLY SPEED*! No need to elaborate here; watch especially for key scratches that create an only speed scenario out of one that would have had a more competitive early pace without the scratch.

2. Improvement – even though a runner's last nine races are terrible! Sudden and significant improvement in both *early* and *final* speeds is a neglected angle by many players; ignore it at your risk.

3. Closely related to improvement: *closers* which win their most recent race convincingly *despite* a slow pace; an indicator of both positive form and perhaps underrated and/or improved ability.

4. Horses that possess an attribute I choose to call "talent." Look for lightly raced, young runners which won first out, then won again in their second career start. Winning the first start and then following with a victory over *winners* is a powerful indication of unusual ability.

5. "Big Win" last race; four or five lengths ahead of the field with trip comments like "Drew away", "In hand", "Clear", "Hand ride"; *and* – importantly – back within a month, good recent works, and winning speed figure that is *not* its top.

6. Again, obvious, dependable, and known to most players; Maiden Special Weight horses dropping into maiden claimers for the first time. The horse should have shown *something* in its MSW race, i.e., some early speed, closing kick, etc. Similarly, and related, *always* check horses dropped into claimers for the first time.

7. I'm always impressed with horses with three or four recent claims, going from one competent trainer to another. In New York, if a horse goes from Jacobson to Rodriguez, to Neville, to Engelhart, that gets my attention.

8. A favorite angle of mine and maybe yours – first race with new trainer – but *not* off a claim! Of course, we don't know the inside story of why a change of trainers was made, but in general, if a horse is given over to a new trainer he or she will want to impress the new connections with a good performance as soon as possible.

9. Another popular angle – small trainer, top rider. Johnny V. riding for Mr. Nobody. Similarly, top riders who take mounts in the last race of the day (ordinary days – not Saratoga or the Kentucky Derby!) deserve a second look. Top jocks often go home early; why did they stick around?

10. And finally, something I've written about before in previous *Horseplayer* articles; *consistency* (I know this conflicts with my "sudden improvement" angle; however, I don't consider them mutually exclusive). A horse who always tries, runs good numbers more often than not, is consistently in the mix, and demonstrates a healthy form pattern, i.e., does not show layoff after layoff in its running lines, is always worth a second look.

So, pay attention when a horse moves to a new trainer; pay attention when "talent" shows in a horse's early running line; but look at each race and each horse holistically, and always ask what may be the most important question of all for handicappers – "Does this scenario make sense?" That "talented" youngster we identified may be entered way over his head today; the "only speed" may have been vanned off in its last race. Any positive angle must be considered in light of the quality of the total field in a given race; simply playing an angle without thorough analysis of each runner is both simplistic and unprofitable.

This a tough game; no quick and easy formulas – but these ten positives are worth a look.

Brisnet's "Ultimate Summary": The Handicapper's Quickie

A**N ONLINE SHOCK** publication called "The Daily Star" recently headlined this story:

> "Sex-mad women flock to Royal Ascot on Ladies' Day for "naughty quirky fun" with strangers…"

Perhaps the "Ultimate Summary" is the handicapper's equivalent of "quirky" if not "naughty" fun.

Let's assume you're hungry for racing action. Work, family, possibly the flu – one or all may have conspired to keep you away from the track or your computer. But today looks better. A little schedule-juggling and you can play the last four or five at your beloved Saratoga; however – no time today for comprehensive handicapping. What to do? The "Ultimate Summary" to the rescue! Here's what it looks like:

| Race Summary | Belmont Park | OC 62500n2x 7 Furlongs 3&up Saturday, June 11, 2016 | Race 13 | E1 E2/Late SPD 96 103/ 94 97 |

13

Exacta; Trifecta (.50); Super (.10) Wagers

7 Furlongs. OC 62500n2x Purse $96,000 (UP TO $17,280 NYSBFOA) FOR THREE YEAR OLDS AND UPWARD WHICH HAVE NEVER WON $10,000 TWICE OTHER THAN MAIDEN, CLAIMING, STARTER OR STATE BRED OR WHICH HAVE NEVER WON THREE RACES OR CLAIMING PRICE $62,500. Three Year Olds, 119 lbs., Older, 124 lbs. Non-winners Of Two Races Other Than Claiming Or Starter In 2016 Allowed 2 lbs. One Such Race In 2016 Allowed 4 lbs. Claiming Price $62,500 (Allowance Horses Preferred)(Non-starters For A Claiming Price Of $25,000 Or Less In The Last 3 Starts Preferred)

Post Time: (7:50)/ 6:50/ 5:50/ 4:50

PARS: E1 E2/LATE SPEED 96 103/ 94 97

ADVANCED FORECAST: Chance Thunderstorms, High 67 Low 64.

RACETYPE STATS:	# Races	FAVORITES Win% ITM% S2ROI	Average Field Size	Median S2 Win Payoff	% Winners < 5/1	% Winners >=5/1 < 10/1	% Winners > 10/1
BEL 3up ALW+ 80000 - 102000 N2X 6.0f-7.0f	22	32% 77% -0.44	7.1	$7.34	77%	18%	5%

Track Bias Stats

	* MEET Totals *					* Week Totals *			
Dirt 7.0f	Speed Bias: 71%		WnrAvgBL		Dirt 7.0f	Speed Bias: 0%		WnrAvgBL	
# Races: 21	04/29 - 06/09		1stCall: 1.8		# Races: 1	06/03 - 06/09		1stCall: 4.7	
%Wire: 33%			2ndCall: 1.6		%Wire: 0%			2ndCall: 6.8	

	Early	Speed	Late	Speed		Early	Speed	Late	Speed
Runstyle:	E ++	E/P	P	S	Runstyle:	E	E/P	P	S +
Impact Values:	1.63	1.07	0.37	0.49	Impact Values:	0.00	0.00	0.00	7.55
%Races Won	43%	29%	10%	19%	%Races Won	0%	0%	0%	100%
Post Bias:	RAIL +	1-3 +	4-7	8+	Post Bias:	RAIL	1-3	4-7 +	8+
Impact Values: Avg Win %	1.12 14%	1.37 17%	0.77 10%	0.79 8%	Impact Values: Avg Win %	0.00 0%	0.00 0%	3.25 25%	0.00 0%

Race Summary

# Horse Name	ML Odds	Med Eqp	Days Since L/R	P Run T Style	Avg Dist/Surf PACE-SPEED S E1 E2/Late Spd	Avg Race Rting	Best Pace E1 E2Late	Final Speed Sp1 Sp2 Sp3 Sp4	Rcg ACL Spd Avg	R1 R2 R3	Mud Spd	Pedigree Stats Mud % Sts Mud	Dam Sire Sire's AWD AWD
10 Watershed	5/2	L	98	S	84 92/105 (100)	116	87 96/110	97. 80 101. 101	114.4 97	118		543 20	7.6 8.1
8 Manhattan Mischief	15/1	L	27	E/P 5	95 103/ 89 * 95"	116	100 105/ 95	96 88. 95. 94	115.7 93	116 117 115	95	170 16	6.7 7.0
5 Dannie's Deceiver	8/1	L	37	P 2	91 98/ 91 * 94"	115	101 102/106	101. 87. 93 87	117.0 94	117 116 114	98	103 20	7.1 7.6
7 Colonel Sharp	12/1	L	30	E 6	102 108/ 82 * 94"	111	103 110/ 82	92 96	112.2 94	112 109		268 17	7.2 6.8
9 Scarly Charly	10/1	L	27	E/P 3	94 100/ 89 * 93"	117	99 103/ 97	94 92. 88	118.1 91	116 117 117	89	687 15	7.0 6.6
2 Amoral	6/1	L	36.	E 7	97 102/ 85 (92)	111	101 106/ 87	95. 100 97 87	115.8 97	116 113 111	100	458 16	7.1 6.9
4 Deep Sea	6/1	L	9.	E/P 2	87 91/ 94 * 91"	115	98 97/103	79† 89 92. 89	113.8 87	116 116 114		834 15	7.3 7.2
6 Cerro	5/1	L	70	E/P 4	94 100/ 82 (91)	116	94 102/ 82	101. 99 96 89	117.0 99	117 117 117	101	1916 14	6.9 8.2
1 Sir Bond	20/1	L	168	P 1	90 97/ 87 (90)	115	96 104/ 98	79 94 93 84	115.7 89	117 116 114	93	520 20	7.2 6.9
11 Between the Lines	30/1	L	27.	P 3	93 106/ 79 * 90"	117	95 106/ 94	85 86 93 98	116.2 88	116 117 117		745 16	6.7 6.5
3 Two Weeks Off	8/1	L	63	E/P 4	93 100/ 74 (83)	116	93 100/ 74	83. 90. 96 89	90	116 119 117		1239 14	7.1 6.8

Speed Last Race	Back Speed	Current Class	Average Class Last 3	Prime Power	Early Pace Last Race	Late Pace Last Race
101 Dannie's Deceiver	101 Dannie's Deceiver	118.2 Manhattan Mischief	121.2 Cerro	142.3 Amoral	119 Amoral	106 Dannie's Deceiver
101 Cerro	101 Watershed	117.8 Dannie's Deceiver	118.3 Watershed	142.0 Cerro	117 Cerro	94 Scarly Charly
96 Manhattan Mischief	100 Scarly Charly	117.5 Scarly Charly	118.2 Amoral	137.2 Colonel Sharp	105 Colonel Sharp	92 Sir Bond
95 Amoral	98 Deep Sea	116.6 Between the Lines	117.8 Dannie's Deceiver	134.9 Scarly Charly	103 Manhattan Mischief	89 Manhattan Mischief
94 Scarly Charly	98 Between the Lines	116.2 Deep Sea	117.0 Scarly Charly	133.8 Dannie's Deceiver	100 Two Weeks Off	82 Cerro
92 Colonel Sharp	97 Amoral	115.6 Colonel Sharp	117.7 Manhattan Mischief	132.9 Two Weeks Off	97 Between the Lines	81 Deep Sea
85 Between the Lines	96 Colonel Sharp	113.7 Two Weeks Off	115.7 Two Weeks Off	131.3 Manhattan Mischief	96 Scarly Charly	81 Colonel Sharp
83 Two Weeks Off	96 Manhattan Mischief	NA Sir Bond	115.6 Colonel Sharp	128.8 Deep Sea	92 Dannie's Deceiver	81 Between the Lines
79 Sir Bond	95 Sir Bond	NA Amoral	115.6 Between the Lines	128.8 Between the Lines	86 Deep Sea	74 Two Weeks Off
79 Deep Sea	91 Cerro	NA Cerro	115.5 Deep Sea	126.3 Sir Bond	79 Sir Bond	71 Amoral
NA Watershed	83 Two Weeks Off	NA Watershed	115.4 Sir Bond	NA Watershed	NA Watershed	NA Watershed

I chose this race at random; however, my experience using the Summary has taught me to avoid maiden races – simply not enough data available. I've been more successful focusing on dirt rather than turf, but the data is there for both. Like all handicappers, I prefer larger fields; eight or more entries.

Let's begin by noting what is *not* included in the Summary: no works, connections, trip information, lifetime starts, lifetime earnings, and no track preference data. It's spare – but it does include the basics. Obviously, if time is *not* a factor, handicappers can supplement Summary data with all or more of the above.

(A personal aside here; when using the Summary, I prefer to limit myself to the data it provides; first, because I only use it when my time is limited and second, I find that if I add all or most of the available *qualitative* data, I'm likely to have "all my ducks in a row" – thus my selection goes off at 4-5!)

Now for a closer look at the data itself. *Horseplayer* readers will find most categories will need little or no further explanation, e.g., track bias data, morning line, days away, running style, the four most recent final speeds, speed last race, early pace last race, late pace last race, and pedigree data.

Other categories will need some explanation:

1. "Average distance/surface pace speed": these are the *average* fractional and final speeds of the horses' most recent races at today's distance and surface. *No* star indicates only one race at this distance and surface, while parentheses warn that the race occurred more than ninety days ago.
2. "Average Race Rating": as I've written elsewhere, Brisnet *quantifies* class; the higher the number, the tougher the fields the horse has been facing.
3. "Best pace" is best pace at *today's* distance and surface within one year.

4. Rcg Spd Avg is average speed in recent races *regardless* of distance or surface.

5. R1, R2, R3 are Brisnet race ratings for a horse's last three races.

6. Back Speed is simply best speed at today's distance and surface within one year.

7. "Av Class Last 3" is the average Brisnet *class* (not race) rating, i.e. how well a horse performs relative to the class of its three most recent races.

8. Current Class is similar to #7, but focuses on races at today's distance and surface.

9. ACL is a unique and intriguing feature of Brisnet's Summary Sheet. In essence, it rates a horse's ability to successfully compete, i.e., to finish *in the money* – against horses at a given competitive level at today's distance and surface. This is a quirky rating - often at odds with the Summary's other ratings – but it sometimes identifies horses at juicy prices.

10. Prime Power: I've saved the best for last. Brisnet's Prime Power Rating is powerful! It combines *dozens* of handicapping features; speed, class, pace, form, weight, and more. I've analyzed hundreds of races over the past four or five years and find it the single-most effective, most accurate comprehensive rating in the Brisnet arsenal – one ignores it at one's peril!

Having said that, a few caveats:

1. A numerical difference may or may not be <u>statistically significant</u>. Meaningful gap advantages for Brisnet's speed ratings are 2-4 points; class ratings 1-2 points; prime power ratings 3-4 points.

2. I have an aversion to *averages*; they often mask a single, strong performance e.g., a top *single* speed figure in the horse's last four races trumps the "average distance surface" for me. Similarly, I downplay the "average class level" rating.
3. The Summary Sheet clearly emphasizes a horse's performance in its most recent races: within ninety days of today's race. A brilliant earlier performance may have been ignored.
4. The Summary Sheet comes down hard on the side of quantitative rather than qualitative data. (Social scientists have argued for decades about their relative merits.) I'm convinced that a consistently successful handicapper needs both; but, on special occasions, the Summary Sheet *is* easily accessible, convenient, and inexpensive.

I've found no numerical formula or particular combination of Summary ratings that produce consistent winners. I'm still experimenting with various combinations; nevertheless, and so far in my long handicapping career, the Brisnet Summary Sheet is the most satisfying "quickie" I've encountered.

Value: A Contrarian's View

I HAVE GOOD friend and fellow handicapper (let's call him "Boris") who is one of the sharpest players I've encountered. He's smart, analytical, experienced, and more importantly, *brave*. Boris has won (and lost) more in one day than I would in a season. He goes to the track with bankrolls of $500-1000 which, considering his income, is possibly comparable to the gambling habits of Ahmed Zayat. (I should mention that, unlike this writer, Boris is also a good *loser*; I suffer pangs of guilt for days after a bad week or two.)

Boris goes to the track to *win*; possibly to someday make that "life-changing score" we hear so much about from horseplayers. Thus, he *takes chances* and often plays against his own analyses, his own obvious choices. Why? He is, of course, looking for prices – for *VALUE*!

Exhibit A: We're standing at the rail on a brisk November day at Aqueduct, comparing notes. Boris mutters (half to himself and half to me) "I like the six horse – he's quicker than anyone in this bunch – no other speed, worked five furlongs in 59 flat last week – can't see any of these outrunning him…"

Ten minutes later, the race is over, the six has won. I congratulate him in his selection. He replies, "I bet the seven…"

"But you *loved* the six…"

"Yeah, but at six-to-five, no value."

(The six incidentally went wire-to-wire in an effortless victory and paid $5.50.)

Boris is of course *conventionally* correct; he's repeating the mantra I read and hear endlessly from players and analysts alike; we must find *value*.

My worst handicapping experience is to tout myself (or be touted by others) *off* a horse my handicapping methods have selected, who of course most likely wins.

Why?

Because I hate being wrong!

Perhaps I suffer from a psychological disorder (some who know me would suggest I suffer from several). Obsessive-compulsive? Perfectionist? Narcissistic?

My expectations are materialistically humble; I don't expect to hit it big, to make that "life-changing score"; but I do expect to get it right often enough to keep me interested in the game; thus I have no problem betting an even money favorite if my analysis tells me he's the obvious choice. I will *not* throw him (or her) out and hunt for a "value" horse. My "value" lies in simply getting it right. (I recognize that I'm oversimplifying the "value" question – i.e., there might well be *value* in my six-to-five selection. However, in my experience, many players are almost automatic in their dismissal of a short-priced runner; I'm *not*.)

I know, of course, that I am swimming against the tide. I am constantly admonished by TV analysts, fellow handicappers, *Horseplayer magazine* and other writers to look for *value*.

My wagers are small – some would describe them as merely token wagers. My selections rarely go off at odds higher than five-to-one. I get as excited as Boris does when my horse is in the midst of a tough stretch duel – even though *he's* rooting for a ten-to-one shot that might yield a $500 or $600 payoff while at best, I'll collect ten bucks.

Fortunately for racing, there are far more Borises than Vin Rogerses and I'm fine with that – I love the game and want it to prosper – so –

Go, Boris! Go for it! May there be value in your every wager – (and a chicken in every pot).

Part IV: At the Track

❖ ❖ ❖

Betting Favorites

TEN OR FIFTEEN years ago, I had a horse with Mitch Friedman named Call Me Anytime. It was Saratoga time, and "Call Me," an honest $35,000 claimer type, was entered in the fifth race on the second Monday of the meet. Come Monday, I made my way to Mitch's barn near the Oklahoma training track. He was relaxing for a moment with a cup of coffee. We chatted for a while and then I asked, "So, how do you think Call Me will do today?"

"He'll piss all over that bunch," he answered.

At post time, Call Me Anytime was the favorite, hovering around even money, 7/5, 8/5…

Headed to the window and bet $200 to win. The race went off: Jorge Chavez was riding. He made a move on the far turn and demolished the field, winning by an increasing six lengths. I happily cashed my $425 ticket.

Now it's commonly accepted among sophisticated horseplayers (including me) that betting favorites is a reliable and dependable way to go broke. But there are times when rules must be broken. My dad made a habit of breaking them.

Uncle Franco

It was the 1940s. The place was Jamaica, New York. My dad was a horseplayer who frequented Aqueduct, Belmont, and the now-defunct

Jamaica track. He was a pharmacist by trade, but everyone called him "Doc." He wanted to be a physician, but the money for medical school just wasn't there, so pharmacy had to do.

His store – a two-pharmacist operation that was much more drugstore than supermarket – was minutes away from where the action was. He'd make weekly visits to the track in season (racing shut down in November and didn't start up again until April), sometimes taking me along.

I was six or seven at the time, and of course, I fell madly in love with everything I saw at the track: the horses, jocks, the silks, the glamour and excitement of the crowds (yes, there were crowds in the 1940s – even on weekdays).

The country was slowly emerging from the deepest depression ever, but my pharmacist dad was doing okay. People needed what he had to sell, and for many he was a substitute for the emergency room. He was, among our struggling extended family, a singular success story. When an aunt, uncle, sister, or cousin needed help, they came to Doc, and he usually delivered, much like a non-violent version of Don Corleone in *The Godfather*. I think he enjoyed that role – reveled in it, in fact – except for occasional challenges from a notorious uncle known only as "Franco."

As I remember it, Uncle Franco had been deported to Italy for crimes short of murder and mayhem but serious enough to warrant deportation. Italy proved to be a fertile ground for his unconventional talents. The rumor, never confirmed, was that he was involved in some aspect of the drug trade. In any case, he prospered, and his wealth and connections enabled him to make periodic visits to the family in the U.S. despite his official deportation.

He would come two or three times a year, stay a week or so, and entertain lavishly: limos, Broadway shows, elegant dining, dollar bills for me and my cousins. My dad was for a little while second banana in the family hierarchy – a role he refused to accept. So shortly after Franco's inevitable departure back to the Old Country, Doc would respond. He'd rent a Long Island beach house and put up everyone for a week or so, or he might pay for a weekend in Atlantic City, which was far more glamorous then than it is now. He'd simply "out-Franco" Franco.

Now, how did he do it? Business was good at the drugstore, but not that good. Doc needed a supplementary source of income to support these expenditures.

Enter Hall-of-Fame trainer "Sunny" Jim FitzSimmons.

"Sunny Jim"

Mr. Fitz trained Gallant Fox, Nashua, and Bold Ruler, among other great thoroughbreds. He won three Derbys, four Preaknesses, and six Belmonts. Brooklyn-born, he lived in Sheepshead Bay for all of his ninety-one years. He was a gregarious native son who really made it big – and, of course, he was one of Doc's heroes (along with "old banana nose" Eddie Arcaro).

One September day during Belmont's fall meeting, Doc settled into his box and discovered that his neighbor was indeed the legendary Sunny Jim – sitting alone with his field glasses at the ready. Doc introduced himself, and the two struck up a conversation. Both Brooklyn-born, they hit it off, and Doc became a welcome visitor to Mr. Fitz's barn.

In fact, Sunny Jim could always count on a visit whenever the infamous Uncle Franco had been in town. Within days of Franco's departure, Doc would show up at the barn, and within a month, he'd get a phone call from someone that went, as I remember it, something like this:

"The boss says that Jiminy Cricket is kicking his stall apart – he looks to be in great shape for the fifth at Aqueduct on Friday."

Or, "Pretty Penny did five furlongs in fifty-nine flat yesterday – she should breeze against that bunch on Saturday."

I'll never know for sure who called, but I do know that after these calls, Doc, usually a $5 or $10 bettor, headed for the track with a stuffed wallet at the ready.

The Jiminy Crickets and Pretty Pennys never went off at anything higher than even money; most were 4/5, even 3/5. Nevertheless, Doc would confidently go to the windows and place $1,000 or sometimes $2,000 to win on Sunny Jim's horses.

This of course would be comparable to my betting $15,000 today – an amount absolutely unimaginable to me. As a university professor, I'd guess my income (adjusted for inflation) might be similar to what Doc's was seven decades ago, but I'd lack both the courage and confidence to do it – not Doc: he had both in abundance, due in part to his complete and utter trust in his good friend Sunny Jim.

So Doc would place his bets early – there was no way he was getting shut out – then he'd go down to the rail and quietly watch his horses run, and *win*, two or three times each year.

Did they ever lose?

I suppose so, but not often enough to offset the stream of winners that came home – almost certainly – from the FitzSimmons barn. Within days of a Fitz-inspired win, Doc would throw a bigger and better party than the upstart Franco, and he'd be the head honcho yet again in town – and he did it all by betting favorites.

HorsePlayer Magazine readers are much too smart to bet their money on short-priced favorites on a daily basis. Indeed, most of us spend our handicapping time figuring out ways to *beat* the favorite. But if Todd Pletcher were my buddy and two or three times a year he told me that one of his horses would "piss all over that bunch" (well, Todd probably wouldn't put it exactly that way!), I think I'd put some significant money on his horse – favorite or not.

The Big Score

MY BIG SCORE is a little different from the others, but nevertheless, I consider it a life-changing event.

When I was 21 or so, I was madly in love with a vivacious blond we'll simply call Susan. I wined her, dined her, did my best to charm her, but so far, she had resisted my efforts to make our relationship a bit more intimate.

One lovely May day, when Belmont's spring meeting had just begun, I suggested we spend a day at the track. She'd been a rider as a girl, and still had that female thing about horses, so she enthusiastically agreed.

It was a weekday – the crowd was light. I bought her a program and a *Form*, began to explain a little about how the game is played. After a Nathan's hot dog and a Coke, we headed to the paddock. The horses were being saddled for the third race. I made what I hoped seemed like informed comments about the horses and their riders.

So far we had simply been absorbing the racetrack atmosphere – I had not placed a bet. Finally she says what I'd hoped she'd say – or something like it – "OK, Mr. Bigtime Handicapper - let's see how good you are. Pick a winner in this race."

"Sure," I replied, "but I tell you what – I'm going to bet something very, very special – a bet just for you."

"Who is it?"

"I'll tell you when the time is right. I'm going to let you wonder about it for a while. Try guessing."

I quickly head for the windows. There's an eight-horse field for the third race. I buy a $10 win ticket on every horse. I put ticket #1 in my upper left jacket pocket, #2 in my inside breast pocket, #3 in my right side pocket, etc., etc.

I return.

"Who *is* it?"

"Not gonna tell you yet – but trust me, I think you're gonna like your horse."

We head for the rail to watch. I exude mysterious confidence. She is puzzled – but intrigued. The horses are in the gate – we hear "They're off!" I watch intently and mutter noncommittal comments like "Come on, baby! – "Yeah! Yeah! Yeah!" As the hit the far turn I yell "Go! Go! Go!" At the 16th pole the winner is obvious. "There he is – there's your horse – the gray, #4!" She squeals with delight as our horse crosses the finish line a comfortable two lengths in front. I reach into my right-side jacket pocket where I know the #4 ticket resides. I flash the ticket, and gallantly hand it to her. The horse pays 21 to 1. I insist that she cash the ticket – about $250. She offers to share. I remind her that this was to be a very special bet on a special horse – just for her. Susan is mightily impressed. Later, I score.

I've Got the Horse Right Here...

REMEMBER THE HIT musical, *"Guys and Dolls"*? Sinatra, Brando – and – for racing fans everywhere - the immortal "Fugue for Tinhorns":

"I got the horse right here, the name is Paul Revere.
And here's a guy that says that if all the weather's clear,
Can do, can do, this guy says the horse can do.
If he says the horse can do, can do, can do."

I've a good friend (actually my girlfriend; she's 74, I'm 89) who is both causal racing fan and well-published writer; thus she is a gatherer – indeed hoarder of words; a connoisseur of language.

Ellen occasionally visited Saratoga with her then husband, Sam. He was into numbers – but Ellen was fascinated by the racetrack culture itself. *He* watched the races – *she* wandered among the stablehands and hot walkers doing their chores in and around the Oklahoma track's sprawling village of grey barns.

In those days, most of New York's daily newspapers included racing information; largely entries and results. The *DRF* provided the hard numbers, the data (no Brisnet, Timeform, Thoro-Graph, Predicteform, Formulator, etc. then).

The Dailys, however short of data, were rife with *opinion;* usually in the form of terse comments following each horse's name in that day's entries.

Ellen, fascinated by their language (essentially, a series of quirky phrases that suggested profundity), was writing a story about "Emma"; a young woman puzzling over her stable of suitors, assessing their pluses and minuses. Many of the handicappers' comments seemed oddly appropriate to her heroine's predicament – thus she jotted down dozens of them in her ever-present notebook which she shared with me a few weeks ago.

My reaction to her list was of course as a *horseplayer* rather than a confused, uncertain lover.

The guys who wrote the racing information for New York's Dailys were clever, canny; this is a tough game – pinpoint accuracy rare or non-existent – but they *must* predict; that's what they're being paid for! Best stance? A kind of vagueness that allows for multiple interpretations – e.g.:

- "Due for wake-up"
- "Unlucky last"
- "Not out of it'
- "Don't ignore"
- "Can be troublesome"
- "Might wake up today"
- "Dangerous here"

Another cluster were more negative – but never *entirely* so – e.g.:

- "Faces tough task"
- "Recent life"
- "Changed hands"

- "Has much to prove"
- "May need one"
- "Not out of it"

Clusters 1 and 2 generally covered 90% or more of a given field – rarely – *very* rarely:

- "Can make no mistakes"

Or, negatively:

- "Hardly the one"

British handicappers incidentally, and predictably, said the same things – but as one might expect, in more poetic language, e.g.:

- "Finished with fair rattle"
- "Showed a clear pair of heels"
- "Gutted, simply gutted"
- "Took the spoils"
- "Quite highly thought of"

I wrote a piece for *Horseplayer* a while ago called "The Big Score." It had to do with my attempt to impress a girl (Susan) I was courting by surreptitiously buying win tickets on every horse in the field – and then, proudly but casually, displaying the winning ticket. Thus in Susan's case, I:

- "Made my presence felt"

and:

- "Managed to take the spoils"

Mostly, however:

- "Never been close"
- "Hardly the one"

were the more accurate assessments.

The Summer of '46

"**V**IN – GET it straight – fifty to *win* – no place, no show. Pauper Prince, sixth race."

"I think I can handle it, Rocco."

Rocco – never Rocky. That was made clear the day we arrived at "The Colony." He was the cook, the undisputed boss of the kitchen – we were the smart-ass college kids' band – George, Bruce, Don, Win, and me - at Cornell, we were known as "Scarlet." We played, we sang, we moved, and we were good enough to be booked for a full summer's gig at this idyllic mountain resort.

The Colony hugged the shores of lovely Loon Lake, deep in the heart of New York's spectacular Adirondack Mountains. The resort included a main building – once the summer retreat of a New York stockbroker – twenty rooms; picture gables, porch, rockers, deerheads on walls; rustic, simple, warm, inviting. A dozen guest cabins surrounded the main house. One – clearly the most decrepit of them all – was reserved for us, the band.

Rocco – single, with no permanent ties to the city – had cooked there for three summers; an old hand. He left the unimaginatively named "Joe's Diner" in the Bronx each June and headed north for a summer in the mountains – and – possibly a female connection or two.

Indeed, many of the Colony's guests *were* single gals trekking north from New York, Boston, or Philadelphia for their annual one or two week vacations; a bevy of nurses, teachers, and secretaries; some looking for Mr. Right – and some simply a summer romance.

Imagine: five single males awash in a sea of guy-seeking females with a new contingent arriving every week. Hey – we would have worked for nothing!

Mid-August, Saturday a.m. A Greyhound bus pulls into the Colony's ample parking lot and disgorges its passengers. We gather (as we did most every Saturday when buses arrived) to assess the newcomers' attributes. One – name Mary Ann – a petite brunette, catches George's eye – and unhappily, Rocco's as well.

Saturday night was big at the Colony. We played a mix of country, blues, and pop – no way you could work if you didn't – but we were jazz players at heart. We finished the first set with something fast and frantic – an up-tempo treatment of Dizzy Gillespie's "Night in Tunisia" – not all that well-received, but we were doing it for us, not them.

Intermission was girlin' time. Our opportunity to act upon the exacting observations we were making as we played our first set.

George – our guitarist – stopped the show night after night with his thoughtful, sensitive solos. While he could swing, he was a killer on ballads. Lithe and athletic, with movie star good looks, the chicks really dug him.

George heads for Mary Ann's table, armed with two summers' worth of move-making experience.

Twenty minutes later, we are back on the stand. "How'd it go, Loverboy?" I ask.

"I'm cautiously optimistic; she digs guitar, but her sister's a nun."

"Challenging, but you can do it."

"I'll give it my best."

"You always do."

The second set goes well; we finish with our irreverent, jazzed up version of Cornell's solemn alma mater – first line's "Far above Cayuga's waters" – maybe you've heard it somewhere.

We pack up our stuff, put horns and guitars in their cases, move the drums out of temptation's way (there's always someone who can't resist a thump or two). We leave the stand; there are nocturnal engagements to be kept.

"You guys stink," Rocco growls, as we head for the exits.

"You're tone-deaf," I reply.

The Rock laughs, begins an animated conversation with George. Later, he saunters off to the bar. I head for the cabin. The sinewy kindergarten teacher from Long Island that I had my eyes on plans to turn in early. It would a quiet night.

George joins me.

"Hi Georgie-Boy, want to go for a swim? Hey – what happened with Mary Ann?"

"Know what that Neanderthal creep said?"

"Mary Ann?"

"Rocco, for Chrissake."

"No, what's on his mind?"

"Wants me to lay off, gives me that maniacal smile and reminds me that I need fingers to play the guitar."

"Forget it, he thinks he's the goddamn Godfather – bark's worse than his bite."

"It's the bite that concerns me."

"Chicken…"

"Screw you."

The Colony was about an hour and half's drive North of Saratoga; glorious Saratoga, the horseplayer and horselover's Mecca – the August place to be.

I got hooked on the sport of kings at six. My dad was a pharmacist; a corner store in Flatbush with a railroad flat apartment upstairs for Dad, Mom, and me. His trade was lucrative enough to allow weekly visits to Belmont, Aqueduct, and the now-defunct Jamaica racetracks. In August, we headed North to the Spa. We stayed at an inn on Lake George – The Antlers – just thirty minutes north of Saratoga. Mom had no interest in the ponies; Dad spent most of *his* time commuting to the track - sometimes he took me along.

We'd go to the paddock and look at the horses close up; inhale pungent barn smells, listen to snorts and whinnies; then watch the jockeys stride majestically toward their mounts. Little guys, of course, resplendent in flaring silks, nonchalantly twirling their whips; all-star athletes, celebrities, and heroes all at once; heady stuff, indeed, for an impressionable six-year-old.

Don, our pianist and fellow punter, came to horseracing from a different place. A native of Worcester, Massachusetts, his family headed West every summer to spend a day or a weekend at the famed Northampton Fair. There were Ferris wheels, cotton candy, hot dogs, 4-H exhibits and – horseracing! No, it wasn't Saratoga. These horses were at the end of their careers; bandaged, taped, their trainers and owners hoping for an in-the-money finish that might pay for hay and the vet for another month or two. But it was racing, and Don, too, was smitten.

Once or twice a week we'd head south to Saratoga for a day at the track. We were free all day, didn't have to be on the stand til 8:00. Rocco, on the other hand, was mired in the kitchen damn near 24 hours a day. Occasionally he'd ask us to place a bet for him. He won a few, lost a lot. So it was with great interest that I examined Pauper Prince's past performances in the Racing Form as we drive down Route 9 on a Friday morning late in August.

"Where the hell did he get this horse?" I mutter as I scan the stats for today's sixth race.

"What horse?"

"Pauper Prince, Rocco's horse. Hasn't raced since March, eased in that one; one work showing 20-1 on the morning line. Why in hell is he betting this clunker?"

"Maybe he's got connections – his Mafia pals in Brooklyn?"

"Yeah, maybe…"

We pull into the parking lot about 10:00. Breakfast at the backstretch kitchen, among grooms and stable hands, listening to racetrack talk - some in Spanish - and study our Racing Forms with an energy and zest that we rarely applied to our books at school.

It's 12:45, almost time for the first race. Optimism abounds. Smiles, laughter everywhere. No one has lost yet.

Don likes a filly - a first-time starter in this five-furlong sprint for two-year-old maidens.

"Who do you like?" Don asks as the horses prance by in the ritual parade to the post.

"The four's lead pony looks like a real threat."

"You gonna lay off this one?"

"I've been known to bet on mice…"

"You're nuts. "

"I like action."

Don's filly finishes up the track.

Things go no better as the day progresses. My horse falls at the first jump of the second race, the only steeplechase on the card. Out of the money in the third and fourth. We decide to skip the fifth to grab a Nathan's hot dog and listen to a swinging jazz trio bravely performing between races for ten or twenty listeners. Most of Saratoga's patrons are there for the races, not the music. Too bad – these guys could play.

We head for the paddock to examine the horses for the sixth, Pauper Prince's race, a seven-furlong sprint. By now I'm out forty-seven bucks – I've got ten left plus Rocco's fifty.

"I like Sonnyboy to win and place. What about you?" Don asks.

"Don't know," I mumble.

I'm staring at Pauper Prince. He doesn't want to be saddled. He rears and begins to show white, foamy sweat between his hind legs. His jock, a wizened journeyman, adequate but no Arcaro, is given a leg up; the horses leave the paddock, head for the track.

Pauper Prince shows 18-1 on the board. _Nobody_ likes him. The Racing Forms' analyst dismisses him with a terse "hardly the one." _This guy is a loser,_ I think – a consistent also-ran. I decide to keep Rocco's fifty. I tuck it firmly into my wallet and we head for the rail in mid-stretch - our favorite viewing place.

"So – made up your mind?" Don asks.

"I'm not betting."

"Been going to Horseplayers Anonymous? When was the last time you laid off two races in a row?...you _did_ bet Rocco's fifty?"

"I'm holding his bet."

"Are you nuts?"

"Man, I may not be great at picking winners, but I know a loser when I see one."

"Maybe – but as Socrates once said, 'That's why they run the races.'"

"You sure Socrates said that?"

"No, but if you told him what you were gonna do, he probably would have…"

Seven furlongs is an awkward distance for most horses - neither a route nor a sprint. Six furlong sprinters often fade during that extra 1/8th of a mile, while routers may need more racetrack to make their closing runs. Pauper Prince is clearly a sprinter – nothing longer than six furlongs showing on his past performances – an unlikely winner even at his best. The crowd enthusiastically agrees and sends him off at 20-1.

"The horses are on the track for today's sixth race," the loudspeaker booms as the eight thoroughbreds prance by the stands. Sonnyboy, Don's horse, decides quite ungraciously to defecate as he trots by (no mean feat, when you come to think about it).

"Did you see that?" Don asks.

"See it? I can smell it."

"I forget – is that a good sign or a bad sign?"

"The poor guy's embarrassed – look at the way he's hanging his head, hoping no one noticed – too humiliated to run well today. I'm afraid you're done..."

"You're full of shit" Don answers.

"No, Sonnyboy is..."

Three minutes til post-time. The track announcer's crisp voice interrupts our conversation. The horses begin their warm-up canters, working their slow and deliberate way to the starting gate.

"How's he look?"

"Who?"

"Pauper Prince, idiot."

Don stares intently through his binoculars for maybe ten or twenty seconds.

"He looks absolutely great, a Cadillac among Fords, a giant among pygmies, Mount Everest among...."

"Give me those glasses, you son-of-a-bitch," I answer, as I yank them away.

Don chuckles, then reassures me that Pauper Prince has no more chance of winning this race than the rotund trumpeter who sounds the call to the post.

"They're in the gate." The announcer's voice is terse, unadorned. The crowd quiets. This is the moment horseplayers relish. For an instant, the world stands still and anything seems possible.

"They're all in line…"

The gates swing open, a bell clangs, the anticipatory silence becomes an excited roar, and the eight thoroughbreds do what they were born to do.

"And they're off…" the announcer continues in his staccato voice.

"That's Pauper Prince going for the lead with By Birdie racing just behind on the rail, followed by Shamrock Green, I'm Okay, and Sonnyboy."

Don and I watch intensely, mildly surprised; Pauper Prince should be laboring along at the back of the pack.

"He'll fade in another furlong," Don assures me.

"Yeah, sure," I answer, still confident, but a little on edge.

"By Birdie ranges up beside Pauper Prince as those two go at it. Shamrock Green is tucked in on the rail a length back; I'm Okay is three lengths behind, then Sonnyboy…"

The announcer continues his call. He's coldly accurate, non-partisan. I hate him for this – but he's not holding a fifty dollar bet on a 20-1 shot that simply can't be allowed to win today. And *he* doesn't have to answer to Rocco.

"That's Pauper Prince and By Birdie battling it out as they hit the turn. They've gone five furlongs in fifty-seven flat."

Now I'm reassured; a fast pace even for stakes horses. By Birdie will exhaust both himself *and* Pauper Prince. A perfect scenario.

"On the turn it's still By Birdie and pauper Prince, with Shamrock green and Sonnyboy starting their moves just three lengths from the leaders…"

"Okay – now's the time to pack it in," I mutter to Don. "Fade, you son-of-a-bitch. Fade," I shout.

"Pauper Prince pokes his head in front; By Birdie continues to battle furiously. Shamrock Green is flying on the outside, followed by Sonnyboy…"

My Racing Form is in shreds; I'm oozing sweat. Everyone else is yelling for *their* horse – I'm pleading for one – *any* one – to make that final, winning burst of speed and save me from disaster.

"By Birdie's through. Shamrock Green is eating up ground on the outside. Pauper Prince is trying to hang on – too close to call! The judges will examine the photograph. Please hold all mutual tickets until the result is official."

"I think Shamrock caught him," Don offers, more out of compassion than conviction.

"You think so?"

I listen to my fellow railbirds' conversation, hoping for some support for Don's view, but opinions are mixed. We wait for the photo.

"Christ, how long does it take to develop a goddamned picture?" I mutter to no one in particular.

Then in three minutes that seemed like an eternity, the announcement…

"The judges have examined the photograph. Pauper Prince is the winner by a nose, with Shamrock Green second and I'm Okay third."

"Oh, shit" I moan.

The numbers go up on the infield board. The race is official. Pauper Prince pays $42.50 for a $2 win bet. I owe Rocco $1,052.50.

"That bastard knew something….his Mafia pals…"

"Maybe, but you gotta make good. What are you gonna do?"

"Don't know…"

"Can your father help?"

"He'd say I got what I deserved for booking bets – man, I'm thoroughly, completely screwed."

"Maybe you can give him fifty a week or something?"

"Yeah – he'll ask how I'm like to die on the installment plan – a finger this week, a toe next week…"

"So what do we do?"

"Don't know – can't go back – can't face him. It's not just the money; it's the total stupidity of it all. This is the dumbest thing I've done in my entire life…"

"No," Don interrupts. "Remember the time you…"

"Shut up."

"I've got to disappear – no other way."

"Yeah? How? Where?"

"I'll go home for now."

"When? You don't have your clothes, your horn, everything's back at the Colony."

"Drive back – I know it's a drag; get as much of my stuff as you can – most of it's in my footlocker."

"It'll take two or three hours…"

"Don – I need you…"

"Okay. What do I tell Rocco?"

"Give him back his fifty. Tell him I got shut out. Hell, it happens – and be sure to get my horn; it's in its case, still on the stand. It's a Bach – worth about a grand. Give it to Rocco - tell him to take it to Schuman's Music on 34th Street. They'll give him a decent price for it; I'll even throw in lessons."

"Funny; he won't be happy."

"Try."

"Okay."

"Don – I need fifty to get home…pay you back as soon as I can."

"Okay."

"Thanks, man."

Don drops me at the Greyhound station – dingy, littered, gloomy; you know what they're like. A Brooklyn-bound bus leaves in three hours. "

I curl up on an empty bench and doze for a while. I awake, stiff, tired, but hungry. Where to eat? No restaurant in sight, but there is a coffee vendor.

I put my money in, the machine disgorges its coffee. I turn and bump into a girl – lithe, curly-haired, barely contained in her Skidmore T-shirt.

"I'm so sorry."

"It's ok."

"Where you headed?"

"Brooklyn," she replies.

Part V: Joey

❖ ❖ ❖

Joey

I JUST LEARNED that Joey died; age, 32. That's not as tragic as it seems since Joey was a horse; and a 32-year-old equine is equivalent to a 90-year-old human.

But – Joey was *my* horse; the seasoned pro who made me a rider.

I got him when he was 14 on the advice of my trainer. He'd seen Joey at numerous local horse shows and knew that this dude could handle the crowd, the noise, and (sometimes) misbehaving and/or aggressive equine competitors; *and* – Joey could jump!

He was small; not quite 16 hands; but agile and smart. A chestnut quarter horse with a white blaze on his head, he was both charmer and athlete. He could effortlessly handle any obstacle under three feet; and since I had no ambitions to jump any higher, we were a perfect match.

One touch of my foot and he'd change leads so smoothly you'd hardly be aware of the switch. Walk, trot, canter, gallop – Joey responded readily to my commands. He was a docile traveler; a pussycat on and off the van.

He'd stand stock-still in the barn while I groomed him; picked his feet, combed his mane and tail, and wrapped his "socks."

An occasional joker, he once picked the crop out of my back pocket as I was leading him back to the barn. When I turned around to open his stall door, there he was with my crop held in his teeth – if horses could laugh, I'm sure he'd have chuckled.

When Joey reached 18 or so, we decided he'd done enough competitive work in the ring; he became semi-retired – i.e., he was *the* horse for all the kids who were about to begin their riding careers. A good number of Windcrest's current adult riders began their riding careers on wise, gentle, obedient Joey.

He never left his home at Windcrest farm. He had a good, kind retirement. I do believe everyone at the barn that knew him loved him.

Another ribbon for my beloved Joey.

In the ring with Joey.

Vin and six-year-old, off-the-track thoroughbred Benny.
(Benny and Joey are barn names.)

Warming up.

Taking a break.

Made in the USA
Middletown, DE
01 December 2017